A NEW BEEF GUIDE

with recipes

100% SCOTCH BEEF

CONTENTS

INTRODUCTION

This book is your definitive guide to everything you need to know about Scotch Beef PGI. Discover why this exceptional red meat is guaranteed to come from animals born and reared only on Scottish farms where animal welfare plays a vital role. This book will give you the confidence and know-how to select, buy and cook Scotch Beef PGI.

It takes time to understand and recognise the different cuts of Scotch Beef PGI that are available. You also need to know how to prepare and cook them perfectly. Whether it is steaks for two, a roast for ten or clever ways to use any leftovers, this book will guide you through what you really need to know. Even if you are an accomplished cook and have some knowledge there may still be something new to learn about Scotch Beef PGI and some new recipes to try.

This book has been produced by Quality Meat Scotland (QMS), the public body responsible for helping the Scottish red meat sector promote Scotch Beef PGI, whilst maintaining the highest standards in Scotland's red meat industry. These standards relate largely to animal welfare, traceability, farming methods, feed and selection and are some of the strictest in the world. When you see the Scotch Beef PGI label in your supermarket, butcher's shop, or restaurant, you can be confident that the meat you are buying is of the highest quality and that's why it should always be your first choice.

ALL ABOUT SCOTCH BEEF PGI

ALL ABOUT SCOTCH BEEF PGI

Nowadays it's only natural to want to know where your food comes from. However, we don't always have time to study the back of every packet we pick up. Luckily, when it comes to choosing fresh or frozen beef, you can simply look for the label that says Scotch Beef PGI to be sure of quality in every bite.

The QMS assurance logos are our shorthand for wholesomeness, safety and taste. Only meat carrying the Scotch Beef PGI logo is guaranteed to come from animals born and reared on assured Scottish farms. Read on to discover what makes this beef so special.

WHAT DOES PGI MEAN?

The PGI (Protected Geographical Indication) logo is your guarantee of an authentic product.

Since 1996 Scotch Beef has held the coveted European Protected Geographical Indication (PGI) status which legally protects it from imitation by meat from outwith Scotland or from products claiming Scotch status. The PGI scheme protects food with a specific heritage.

To look at a full list of PGI products check http://ec.europa.eu/agriculture/quality/schemes/index_en.htm

WHAT IS THE DIFFERENCE BETWEEN SCOTCH AND SCOTTISH?

In a nutshell, **Scotch Beef PGI** is sourced from selected Scottish farms that must meet stringent criteria regarding animal welfare, feeds and natural production methods. We believe that our selection criteria lead to the best possible traditional tasting beef.

Only approved farms and processors based in Scotland can produce Scotch Beef PGI. Not all beef from Scotland is eligible to use the name Scotch Beef PGI.

Scottish beef refers to any cattle that have been born, reared and processed in Scotland independent of any quality guarantees. It holds no PGI status.

WHAT IS THE SCOTCH BEEF PGI ASSURANCE SCHEME?

A whole chain assurance programme with the benefit to reassure you that the Scotch Beef you buy is authentic and the best it can be.

It is the longest established scheme of its kind in the world, and celebrates a milestone 25th anniversary in 2015.

This whole of life brand eligibility is delivered by a suite of assurance schemes: one livestock: Cattle & Sheep and four non livestock: Feeds, Haulage, Auction Market and Processor.

Whole chain assurance underpins the integrity of Scotch Beef PGI. It provides reassurance of provenance, highest standards of production, animal welfare and wellbeing, to deliver a quality eating experience.

As well as being born and reared for all its life on a Scotch assured farm and processed in an approved establishment, to ensure the best consistent eating quality we only select the best prime cattle:

- no old cows or old bulls
- over 12 months of age
- under 16 months if a young bull
- under 48 months if a steer or a heifer

Our quality selection criteria don't end at the farm gate. To ensure that only the best Scotch Beef PGI reaches your table the Scotch Beef PGI standards include proper selection and classification of carcases and the chilling process.

BUY WITH CONFIDENCE

You can be sure that whenever you buy Scotch Beef PGI that it's the genuine article. It has been quality assured for its whole life in Scotland; the farm and processor have been independently audited to make sure they meet stringent requirements regarding animal welfare and natural production methods. This all means that the Scotch Beef PGI you buy is fully traceable back to its farm of origin.

ANIMAL WELFARE AND WELLBEING

The QMS Welfare and Wellbeing Charter recognises the five freedoms of animal welfare and wellbeing and is a guiding principle for all QMS assurance schemes that are supported by the Scottish SPCA, Scotland's independent animal welfare charity. The Scottish SPCA also carries out some joint visits to QMS approved livestock farms along with Scottish Food Quality Certification (SFQC) farm assessors. *(For more information on the five freedoms of animal welfare see www.qmscotland.co.uk).*

Many cattle produced in Scotland originate from herds that are uniquely acclimatised to the farms they are reared upon. Young cattle normally suckle their mother for at least the first six months, forming a strong bond with each other and the farm.

SUSTAINABLE FARMING PRACTICES

Extensive grass-based system –
Scotland's livestock production systems
are based on free ranging livestock
grazing at low stocking densities and
eating grass and forage from land often
unsuitable for growing alternative
food sources. This largely avoids the
diversion of protein, suitable for human
consumption, into the production of
livestock. Permanent grass and rough
grazing account for about 80% of Scottish
agricultural areas where it would not be
possible to produce any other food other
than livestock *(Source: Scottish Government)*.

Welfare is a priority – The industry
works very closely with the Scottish
SPCA (Scotland's animal welfare charity).
Scottish SPCA inspectors regularly visit
our farms and animal health is also a
priority in Scottish livestock production.

Abundant water supply – In Scotland
the water cattle drink is not diverted from
human use. The ample supply of rain
creates lush grassland which is ideal for
the natural production of livestock.

Encouraging diversity – Livestock
production plays an important part in
sustaining the diverse landscape for which
Scotland is famed. Scotland's hill livestock
farmers typically farm both cattle and
sheep, a mixed grazing system which
benefits landscape biodiversity *(Source:
Scottish Natural Heritage)*.

Beef breeds – A typical Scotch Beef PGI
farming system involves suckler cows (beef
breeds farmed to produce beef rather
than milk) farmed on low input grassland.
This type of farming is critical to the
maintenance of many hill and upland
habitats.

Reducing carbon emissions – Through
restructuring and farm efficiency
improvements the Scottish red meat
industry has succeeded in reducing its
carbon emissions and waste. Carbon
emissions in Scotland for agriculture and
related land use reduced by 27% between
1990 and 2010. *(Source: National Atmospheric
Emission Inventory)*. The industry continues
to strive to further improve efficiency and
reduce waste.

Grassland's role in carbon capture
– Hill and upland farms in Scotland
play a substantial role in improving the
environment through the removal of CO_2
from the atmosphere. This capturing
and storing of carbon is known as
sequestration. *(Source: QMS R&D Report
2011/12)*.

Hormone free – Scotch Beef PGI is free
from artificial growth hormones.

Antibiotic and other residue – Just
like humans, cattle can sometimes fall
ill and are prescribed drugs from a vet
to make them better. Only therapeutic
drugs are prescribed for welfare reasons.
The quality scheme monitors the use
of these drugs to avoid residue entering
the food chain. The withdrawal period
for medicine residue must be completed
before the animal enters the food chain.

SOCIAL SUSTAINABILITY

Social heritage – Livestock production has played a key role in Scotland's social heritage for centuries. Cattle and sheep farming remains at the heart of rural communities throughout the country.

Farming families – Scottish livestock farms typically remain in the same family for generations allowing farming skills to be passed down by family members. This includes invaluable knowledge of the terrain and conditions as well as animal care skills.

Sustaining jobs – Around 50,000 jobs in Scotland depend on the Scottish red meat industry. Many of these jobs sustain employment in fragile rural communities.

A HEALTHY BALANCE

Scotch Beef PGI can be an excellent source of nutrients. Here are some good to know facts:

- Red meat is a source of protein which is essential for energy and the body's growth and repair.

- It is also a source of iron and contains high quality haem iron that is easily absorbed by the body.

- Red meat contains zinc, which is needed for muscle recovery and contains B vitamins which are known to support immune function.

- Raw meat contains virtually no salt and by cooking from scratch you can control your intake.

- Enjoy red meat as part of a balanced diet, including at least five portions of fruit and vegetables every day.

For more information visit:
www.food.gov.uk

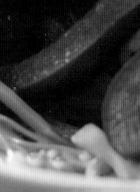

MEAT CHARACTERISTICS

FACTORS AFFECTING THE TENDERNESS OF MEAT

The farm is the vital first stage in the supply chain, and from the day the animal is born, key decisions are made here that will, during the course of its life, define the eating quality of its meat.

QMS and Scotland's farmers are tirelessly committed to close adherence and constant review of the very best farming practices:

- Feeding and management to achieve constant and acceptable growth rates.
- Careful handling and transportation of animals.
- Minimising mixing of unfamiliar animals.
- Ensuring consistent growth.
- Avoiding slaughter soon after diet changes.
- Best animal genetics selected for the local environment.

Animal welfare is good for meat quality as well as for the animals.

AGING AND HANGING

Carcases are held in refrigerated storage for varying periods of time to improve eating quality. Beef was traditionally suspended on hooks by the Achilles tendon, however, more recently, suspending them from the hip via the hole in the bone called the aitch-bone has been recommended. It allows hanging in a more natural way and prevents muscles being stretched artificially. Aitch-bone hanging develops these muscles in such a way as to offer better meat eating qualities for the end-customer. Recommended time intervals between slaughter and retail sale for hindquarter beef with aitch-bone suspension are at least 7 days, up to 21 days for better eating quality.

STORING MEAT

It's important to store raw meat correctly in your fridge to stop bacteria from spreading and avoid food poisoning.

Store raw meat in clean, sealed containers on the bottom shelf of the fridge, so it can't touch or drip onto other food.

Follow any storage instructions on the label.

Keep cooked meat separate from raw meat.

For more information contact the Food Standards Agency or visit their website, ***www.food.gov.uk***

MEAT COLOUR

Depending on certain atmospheric conditions, red meat can change colour quite significantly and appear anywhere between bright red and dark brown. This is due to concentrations in the air of various gases which react with a pigment in the meat called myoglobin.

When meat is first cut from the carcase, it's a purplish-red colour because it hasn't been exposed to oxygen. It is the meat's reaction with oxygen that turns it bright red. Red is good for beef, but slightly browner meat will often have a better taste and flavour.

The brown colour comes from being further exposed to oxygen and it's one of the signs of a well-aged piece of beef. Far from meaning the meat is going off, this colour is a natural part of the meat maturing – something that releases wonderful flavours.

If you purchase your meat in a vacuum-pack or skin pack the meat often appears to be a darker red, make sure you open the pack a good 20 minutes before cooking to allow the meat to come back to its full colour.

MARBLING

As well as the external layer of fat just beneath the surface of the skin, there is another fat present in animals known as 'marbling'.

Fat is critical to the flavour of meat and helps differentiate one meat from another. In fact, research has shown that if all traces of fat are stripped from a piece of beef and a piece of lamb, it is almost impossible to tell them apart. Marbling develops over time so is more predominant in beef than lamb or pork. In short, marbling is small streaks of intramuscular fat that are found in the muscle. It has a beneficial effect on juiciness and flavour by 'melting' through the meat during the cooking process.

CUTS AND COOKING

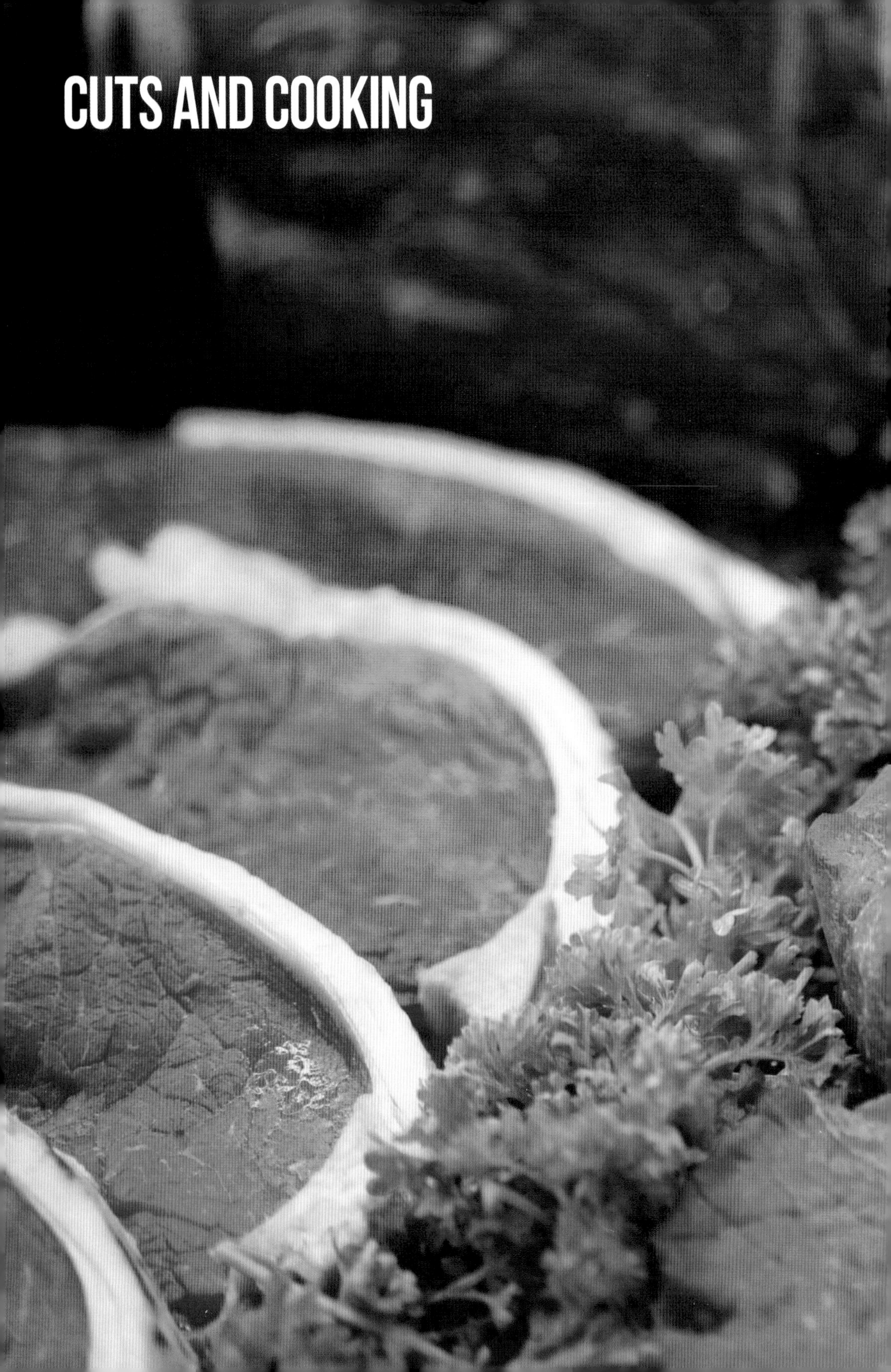

CUTS AND COOKING

CHOOSING THE RIGHT CUT OF BEEF

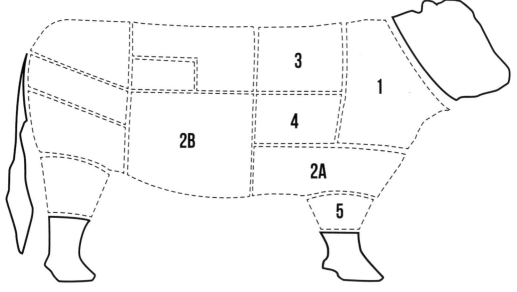

SCOTCH BEEF PGI FOREQUARTER

The versatility of Scotch Beef PGI is as infinite as your imagination. Due to the variety of cuts that Scotch Beef PGI offers, the range of dishes you can prepare is huge. However, because of this flexibility, all beef is not the same: different cuts require different cooking.

You don't need to buy prime sirloin to enjoy Scotch Beef PGI at its best – the secret to a great meal is in how you prepare the different cuts of meat. Knowing how to cook some of these less well-known cuts will give you a head start when it comes to exploring new recipes using Scotch Beef PGI.

The information in the next few pages is a comprehensive snapshot of the most commonly used and prepared cuts.

1. NECK AND CLOD

Products: Diced.

Cooking methods: Stewing, casseroling and braising.

2A. BRISKET 2B. FLANK

Products: Flank steak (bavette, skirt), roasting joints and short ribs.

Cooking methods: Ideal for moist, slow heat including stewing, braising and pot roasting. Also excellent for curing.

3. CHUCK/BLADE/FORERIB

Products: Roasting joints and steaks, (ribeye) when properly trimmed.

Cooking methods: Ideal for slow cooking such as casseroling, pot roasting, braising and slow roasting.

4. LEG OF MUTTON/THICK RIB

Products: Diced, steaks (thinly sliced and served rare only to avoid poor eating experience).

Cooking methods: Frying, stewing, grilling and casseroling.

5. FORE SHIN

Products: Shin.

Cooking methods: Stewing, casseroling (ideal for osso buco, Italian for 'hollow bone'). The end of the animal's front legs, the shin, is generally inexpensive. It should be given plenty of time to cook slowly and can be obtained either on or off the bone. Enjoy the marrow in the bone – a continental delicacy.

OFFAL

Products: Liver, kidneys, oxtail, cheeks, tongue, heart and tripe.

Cooking methods: Ideal for moist, slow cooking – stewing and casseroling to produce tender results. Liver is best when fried quickly.

CUTS AND COOKING

CHOOSING THE RIGHT CUT OF BEEF

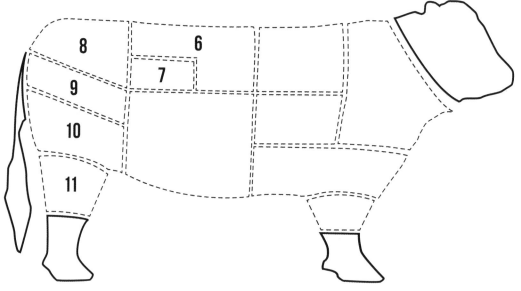

SCOTCH BEEF PGI HINDQUARTER

The hindquarter provides the majority of tender steak cuts; fillet, sirloin and T-bone as well as the classic roasting joints, silverside, topside and rump.

6. LOIN

Products: The loin is made up of various ribs which are well known as steaks e.g. sirloin, porterhouse, T-bone etc. A T-bone is a sirloin steak left on the bone with fillet attached.

Cooking methods: All generally are suitable for higher temperature methods of cooking such as pan frying, grilling or roasting.

7. FILLET

Products: Cut into steaks or roasted whole.

Cooking methods: Grill, pan fry or roast. Fillet trimmings from the head, tail or chain are great for stir-frying or for a stroganoff. Add slivers to make tasty Thai beef soups.

8. RUMP/POPESEYE

Products: Roasting joints or sliced into steaks. Pavé (French for paving stone and referring only to the shape) – is often used to describe a trimmed piece of rump that is very uniform and rectangular in shape.

Cooking methods: Rump is made up of several very different muscles e.g. rump cap, rump heart (or eye) and rump tail. These muscles do vary in tenderness and can be cooked as roasts or sliced into high quality steaks. Rump heart being the most tender.

9. TOPSIDE

Products: Roasting joints of various sizes.

Cooking methods: Topside is generally roasted. Suitable for either dry or wet roasting.

10. SILVERSIDE

Products: Roasting and curing in joints of various sizes.

Cooking methods: Silverside is another slow cooking or carvery joint. It is very lean and sometimes has a layer of pre-formed fat added to prevent the meat becoming too dry during cooking. Silverside is ideal for curing or salting. This can be either wet or dry cured using salt and a mixture of spices.

11. HIND SHIN

Products: Hough and shin.

Cooking methods: Stewing, casseroling or confit. Shin, also known as leg of beef, is rich in collagen and connective tissue and has delicious marrow running through the hollow centre of the bone. It is essential to cook slowly at lower temperatures with plenty of moisture that will make a rich tasty sauce. Cut right through the bone, it is perfect for osso buco. Cook slowly on or off the bone until the meat falls away and press into a mould to make traditional Scottish potted hough.

COOKING METHODS
AND TIMES

COOKING METHODS AND TIMES

FRYING/GRILLING STEAK

There are many different cuts of steak to choose from, more than just fillet and sirloin; ribeye, rump, popeseye, T-bone, minute, bavette.

Basic Method

Remove steaks from the fridge at least 15 minutes before cooking to allow the meat to come to room temperature. This will enhance their tenderness after cooking.

Always preheat the grill or pan before starting to cook the steak.

Pat with kitchen paper to ensure steaks are dry before rubbing with oil on both sides and then season it with salt and black pepper. Try using groundnut oil as an alternative to other oils as it can withstand high temperatures without burning.

Don't over handle the steak. Try to limit the turning to only once – halfway through cooking. Finally, allow the meat to rest for at least 3 minutes after cooking.

Timings are approximate – based on a 1" thick sirloin steak, pan fried. *(See opposite page).*

Get your steaks and roasts right first time using the "Perfect Steaks and Roasts" app available from the App Store or Google Play. Download these free, easy to follow instructions which will help you make a succulent steak or a roast that will be cooked to complete perfection.

BLUE
Seared outside, 1 min each side
100% red centre
Internal temp: 10-29°C

RARE
Seared outside, 2½ mins each side
75% red centre
Internal temp: 30-51°C

MEDIUM/RARE
Seared outside, 3-4 mins each side
50% red centre
Internal temp: 57-63°C

MEDIUM
Seared outside, 4 mins each side
25% pink centre
Internal temp: 63-68°C

MEDIUM/WELL
5 mins each side
Slight hint of pink
Internal temp: 72-77°C

WELL DONE
6 mins each side
100% brown throughout
Internal temp: 77°C+

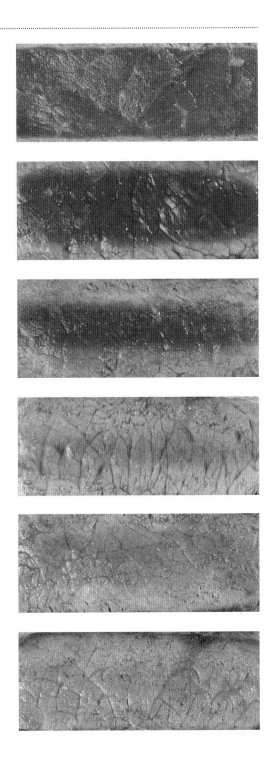

TOUCH TEST

The easiest way to test how cooked your steak is, is to press on the meat with your fingertips.

Press on the meat here and there while it cooks, and compare the feeling of the meat with the following finger test. You'll get better with practice.

RAW

Open the palm of your hand. Relax the hand. With your other index finger push on the fleshy area between the thumb and the base of the palm. This is what raw meat feels like.

RARE

Press the tip of your index finger to the tip of your thumb. The fleshy area below the thumb should give quite a bit. This is what rare meat feels like. Open up your palm and compare raw to rare.

MEDIUM/RARE

Gently press the tip of your middle finger to the tip of your thumb. Feel the flesh beneath the thumb. This is what medium rare meat feels like.

MEDIUM

Press the tip of your ring finger and your thumb together. The flesh beneath the thumb should give a little more. This is what medium cooked meat feels like.

WELL DONE

Gently press the tip of your pinky and thumb together. Again feel the fleshy area below the thumb. It should feel quite firm. This is what well done meat feels like.

ROASTING

Cooking a roast is the perfect solution as it allows you time to prepare other dishes, vegetables and any sauces while the meat is happily cooking. Traditional dry roasting is simply a great way to cook larger, tender cuts of meat – such as rib, ribeye, sirloin, rump and topside.

Less tender cuts such as silverside, brisket, chuck, featherblade and shin can also be roasted but require additional moisture and longer, slower cooking – usually covered all or part of the cooking time – this is sometimes called pot roasting (see page 36).

Quantity

The current recommended daily intake of red meat is around 70g cooked weight per person. Even at lower temperature cooking, around 20% shrinkage will occur, so allow approximately 120g raw meat per person if the joint is boneless and approximately 225g if the meat is on the bone. When calculating how much to buy, always add a little extra – a larger piece of meat will cook better and cold roast beef can make any number of meals for later in the week (see pages 40 and 60).

Basic Roasting Method

The following simple instructions use a lower roasting temperature to minimise the loss of moisture and shrinkage caused by cooking at higher temperatures.

Allow the meat to come to room temperature and ensure that it is completely dry before cooking.

Preheat the oven to 180°C (or turn down to 180°C if the meat has been browned in a very hot oven, see following).

Brown the meat, either in a hot pan with a little vegetable oil or in a very hot oven at 220°C for 15 minutes.

Once the meat has been browned, place it uncovered on a wire rack in a shallow roasting tin, ensuring that any fat is on the top.

Continue to cook at 180°C until it has reached the required internal temperature, or level of 'doneness'.

Timing

The formula for roasting meat is based on minutes spent in the oven per kilo of meat. Weigh the piece of meat before cooking and calculate the cooking time. If you are roasting a stuffed joint – weigh after stuffing. Use a skewer to test the juices' colour to indicate what stage the meat is at – red (rare), pink (medium) and clear (well done).

After the roast comes out the oven, cover it with foil, (shiny side down) and allow it to rest for at least 10-15 minutes. This allows the meat to relax so the juices become evenly distributed throughout, making it more succulent and easier to carve.

See page 139 for the "Perfect Steaks and Roasts" app.

RARE
Juices are red
Allow 15-20 minutes
per 450g
+ extra 20 minutes

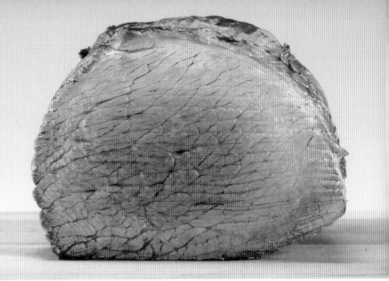

MEDIUM
Juices are pink
Allow 21-25 minutes
per 450g
+ extra 20 minutes

WELL DONE
Juices are clear
Allow 26-30 minutes
per 450g
+ extra 20 minutes

POT ROASTING

Less tender cuts, such as brisket, can also be roasted but require additional moisture and longer, slower cooking – usually covered for all or part of the cooking time.

Basic Pot Roasting Method

Brown the piece of meat as the basic roasting method (*see page 34*) and place in a deep casserole/braising dish with vegetables, herbs and seasoning to add extra flavour.

Root vegetables, such as onion, carrot, turnip, celeriac, leek, celery and potato are perfect accompaniments and should be roughly cut into large chunks that will not break up during cooking. Mushrooms, peppers and tomatoes are also great but should be added when there is still 40 minutes of cooking time remaining.

Allow approximately 450g vegetables and 150ml liquid, which can be water, stock, wine, cider, beer or a mixture for a 1.25kg joint.

Cover tightly and cook slowly. Allow 30-40 minutes per 450g plus an extra 20 minutes.

SLOW COOKER

This is a great way to cook food when you are short of time and want a meal ready when you need it.

Stews and casseroles are ideal to slow cook.

Remember that the liquid won't evaporate or thicken during cooking, so if you're adapting a standard recipe, it's best to reduce the liquid by roughly a third. Liquid should just cover the meat and vegetables. You can also use a teaspoon of cornflour mixed to a paste with a little cold water to thicken the stew toward the end.

Ingredients will cook at different speeds, always check your manufacturers guidelines on when to add ingredients.

USUAL COOKING TIME	SLOW COOKING TIME
15-30 mins	1-2 hours on high 4-6 hours on low
30-60 mins	2-3 hours on high 5-7 hours on low
1-2 hours	3-4 hours on high 6-8 hours on low
2-4 hours	4-6 hours on high 8-12 hours on low

CASSEROLES

Casseroles are a great dish that can be served all year round. They are economical and an excellent way to cook meat and vegetables together. Predominantly cuts for casseroling come from the forequarter *(see page 24-25)*. They are quick to prepare, freeze well and require little attention during cooking. Once you master the basics, the variations are endless.

Basic Casserole Method

If your meat is not already cubed, remove any fat and cut into bite sized cubes.

Place in a plastic bag and add plain seasoned flour (1 tablespoon per kilo of meat). Toss until the cubes of meat are completely coated. The flour will thicken the sauce during cooking.

Heat a dessert spoon of vegetable oil in a large flameproof casserole dish or frying pan until very hot.

Brown the cubes by adding a few pieces at a time to the hot dish. Do not add too many at one time. Remove the browned meat from the dish and set aside before browning the next batch.

Sauté any fine cut vegetables such as onions, shallots and leeks then remove from the dish.

Add 200ml of liquid. This could be meat or vegetable stock, red wine, beer, cider or even water. Use this to dissolve the cooking juices and loosen the meaty residues from the bottom of the pan. This is called deglazing and is the basis for many sauces.

Place the browned meat and the sautéed vegetables back into the casserole dish; add some chunky, chopped seasonal root vegetables; season; pour over the deglazing liquid and additional stock so half the meat is covered and bring to a simmer.

Put the lid on the casserole dish and place in a preheated oven around 140°C and cook for between 2-3 hours or until the meat is tender.

Know your oven. Gas and electric cooking times are similar, but the age and the size of your oven can affect cooking times.

BBQ'ING

Barbecue basics

The smell and taste of a sizzling BBQ are hard to beat. Whether you're having an intimate BBQ with close friends and family or feeding the masses at a party, it's the perfect occasion to enjoy the great taste of Scotch Beef PGI.

Why not do your cooking outdoors, even if the weather isn't perfect, cook out and eat in! Alternatively, use the grill then you can sizzle whatever the weather.

Great Grillers

Cuts that work best on the BBQ are those which work well when cooked quickly, like frying or grilling, for example:

Steaks – Fillet, sirloin, ribeye, rump, popeseye, T-bone and sirloin extra thin/minute steak.

Cubed – Good lean braising steak, topside, ribeye or sirloin.

Minced – Mince is perfect for making burgers or sausages.

Be safe

- Wash your hands thoroughly before and after handling raw meat.
- If using charcoal, ensure it is very hot – grey and powdery, before cooking.
- Use separate utensils and plates for cooked and raw meat.
- Charred doesn't mean well done – even if meat is burnt on the outside, it might not be cooked inside. Cook food over a steady heat and always check it's cooked in the centre and is piping hot.
- BBQ's can be dangerous – please take necessary precautions to avoid burns, fires and food poisoning.

For more food hygiene information visit **www.food.gov.uk**

The original fast food

Summer cooking is about using cuts of meat that cook quickly, whether frying, griddling or BBQ'ing. Below is a guide to some of the best known cuts and how long they take to cook.

Cooking times

BEEF STEAKS	COOKING TIMES
Fillet, sirloin, ribeye, rump, popeseye, T-bone, sirloin extra thin/minute steak	Rare – seared outside, $2^{1}/_{2}$ mins each side. Medium – seared outside, 4 mins each side. Well done – 6 mins each side.
DICED BEEF KEBABS	**COOKING TIMES**
Lean braising steak, topside, ribeye or sirloin	Use even sized cubes of meat, cook for 10-15 minutes. Turn and brush regularly with a marinade or oil until done to your liking. Rest the kebabs for at least 5 minutes before eating.
MINCED CUTS	**COOKING TIMES**
Burgers	Burgers about 2cm thick, cook for 6-7 minutes on each side.
Sausages	Medium to thick sausages, cook for about 10-15 minutes turning regularly.

Note: Cooking times will vary depending upon the thickness of the cut. Dry meat with kitchen paper before cooking.

CARVING TECHNIQUES

There are two methods of carving boned
and rolled joints. Either lay the piece on its
side and then cut slices from it almost as
if it was a loaf of bread, or you may prefer
to position it so that the round surface is
horizontal and then carve across the grain.

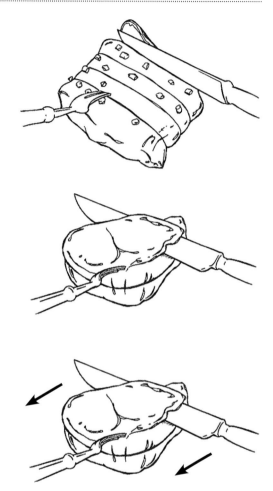

To do this place the joint so that the
round surface is vertical and insert the
fork into the curved side nearest to you,
or, if particularly long, it might be easier
to insert nearer the middle and carve
from the far end. When the remaining
piece is too thin and 'wobbly' to carve,
lay it down so that the round surface is
horizontal (facing upwards), inserting the
fork into the side nearest to you and carve
slices across the grain, increasing the
angle as you come to the end*.

Always cut across the grain.**

* Take great care when carving like this,
if unsure carve away from your body.

** The grain is the collection of muscle
fibres in a piece of meat and the direction
they run in, these fibres are visible.

RECOMMENDED COOKING TIMES FOR BEEF

CUT	COOKING	TEMPERATURE	TIMING
Sirloin, Fore rib, Topside, Silverside, Ribeye, Rump/ Popeseye	Roast	180°C 350°F Gas mark 4-5	**Rare** – 20 mins per 450g plus 20 mins **Medium** – 25 mins per 450g plus 20 mins **Well done** – 30 mins per 450g plus 20 mins
Brisket	Pot roast or slow roast	180°C 350°F Gas mark 4-5	30-40 mins per 450g plus
Stewing shoulder, Steak hough	Stew/casserole	170°C 325°F Gas mark 3	2-3 hours
Prime casserole, Thick flank	Casserole	170°C 325°F Gas mark 3	1-1½ hours
STEAKS			
Popeseye/Rump, Sirloin, Ribeye	Grill/fry	N/A	**Rare** – 2 mins each side **Medium** – 4 mins each side **Well done** – 6 mins each side
Sirloin extra thin	Grill/fry	N/A	1 min each side
Fillet	Grill/fry	N/A	**Rare** – 3-4 mins each side **Medium** – 4-5 mins each side **Well done** – 6-7 mins each side

Note: Cooking times will vary depending upon the thickness of the cut.

LEFTOVERS AND PLANNING MEALS

MAKE ANOTHER MEAL OF IT

Buying what you need while it's fresh and in season is not only a great way to experience the very best quality produce, it can also maximise your shopping budget.

There is so much more to Scotch Beef PGI than a one-off roast dinner. Maybe it is just the delicious taste of the meat itself, or the cooking method, but one thing is certain, leftover roasts can taste even better second time around.

To make the most of every last piece, leftovers can be used for dinners, lunches, light meals or snacks. Excellent in curries, salads and sandwiches, pasta and rice dishes, soups and stocks.

Basic stock recipe

Meat bones make the best flavoured stock and although time consuming it is absolutely worth it. You can use every last piece of meat and bones to help flavour the stock, there is no waste whatsoever. You can then freeze the stock in small portions to use as needed.

You will need: 900g beef bones, 2 sprigs of thyme, 2 sprigs of parsley, 1 large bay leaf, 2 onions, roughly chopped, 2 celery sticks, roughly chopped, 2 carrots, roughly chopped, 5 peppercorns.

Place the bones in a large saucepan and add about 2 litres of water, enough to cover the bones. Bring to the boil, skimming off the scum as it rises to the surface.

Tie the thyme, parsley, bay leaf into a bouquet garni and add to the pan with the onions, celery, carrots and peppercorns. Cover and simmer gently for 5-6 hours.

Strain the stock through a sieve into a bowl, discarding the bones and vegetables. Leave to cool, then chill until the fat has risen to the surface of the stock and solidified. Lift the fat off the surface and discard before using the stock.

Further stock ideas

To make a richer, brown stock, roast the bones in a hot oven (230°C) for 40 minutes.

For a boneless stock, brown a 125g piece of stewing beef in 1 tablespoon sunflower oil in a large saucepan. Remove the meat, and add a roughly chopped onion, carrot and celery stick to the pan. Brown the vegetables, then pour in 2 litres of water and bring to the boil. Add the meat and heat until simmering again, skim off any fat, add 2 bay leaves, a sprig of parsley and thyme, 10 black peppercorns and $\frac{1}{2}$ tsp salt. Reduce the heat, cover and simmer for 2 hours. Strain, cool and remove any fat. This will make about 1.2 litres of stock.

After chilling the stock you can boil it until reduced and concentrated in flavour, then cool and freeze it. Ice-cube trays are a great way to store stock then you can simply add them frozen to your hot soup, casserole or stew and they will melt in with all their lovely flavours. Taste constantly to check the correct strength of flavour has been achieved, it's easy to add an extra frozen cube of stock as you go.

FREEZER FRIENDLY

Save time, work and money by making extra portions for the freezer to help plan weekly meals. Mince, stew and casserole dishes are perfect for freezing. Invest in some good freezer containers, make sure you label and date food clearly so there is no guessing what's inside.

Storing and freezing

There are a few straightforward rules you should follow to use leftovers and freeze cooked food safely;

- Cool then store leftovers in the fridge as quickly as possible. Cover them well and eat within 2 days.

- If freezing, cool thoroughly first. Once frozen they will keep indefinitely, but the quality will deteriorate so try to eat them within 3 months.

- Defrost leftovers completely. Ideally in the fridge overnight, or defrost in the microwave if you want to cook straightaway.

- Eat leftovers within 24 hours of defrosting and do not refreeze.

- Ensure leftovers are cooked until completely hot throughout.

For further advice on storing and reheating food visit *www.food.gov.uk*

ROAST RECIPES

BEEF & ALE POT ROAST

SERVES: **6**   PREP: **10 mins**   COOK: **2 hrs 10 mins**

INGREDIENTS

1.25kg lean Scotch Beef PGI brisket, boned and rolled

1 tbsp oil

2 red onions, peeled and quartered

6-8 baby carrots, peeled

4 sticks celery, cut into chunks

2 bay leaves

Salt and black pepper

450ml beef stock

150ml brown ale

1-2 tbsp gravy granules

METHOD

1. Preheat the oven to 170°C.

2. Heat the oil in a large saucepan, add the joint and brown all sides.

3. Place in a deep 3.4 litre (6 pint) ovenproof casserole. Arrange the onions, carrots, celery and bay leaves around the joint and season well. Add the stock and brown ale. Cover with a tight fitting lid and cook for 2 hours.

4. Thicken with gravy granules if desired.

5. Serve joint, cut into thick slices, with braised vegetables and new potatoes.

ROAST TOPSIDE OF SCOTCH BEEF PGI

SERVES: **6** PREP: **15 mins** COOK: **1 hr 45 mins (approx)**

INGREDIENTS

1.5kg Scotch Beef PGI topside. You can ask your butcher to coat the joint with extra fat to keep the meat moist during roasting.

3 red onions, peeled and quartered

6 medium carrots, peeled and cut into chunks

1 butternut squash, peeled and cut into chunks

1 garlic bulb, peeled and cloves separated

2-3 tbsp olive oil

Salt and black pepper

A few sprigs of thyme

COOKING TIMES

Rare:
15-20 mins per 450g plus 20 mins

Medium:
21-25 mins per 450g plus 20 mins

Well Done:
26-30 mins per 450g plus 20 mins

METHOD

1. Preheat the oven to 220°C. Rub the beef with 1 tablespoon olive oil and season with salt and pepper, rub all over. Put the beef in a roasting tin in the hot oven for 15 minutes to brown.

2. Place all the vegetables and thyme in the roasting tray around the meat and drizzle them with 1 tablespoon olive oil. Put the roasting tray back in the oven. Turn down the heat to 180°C and cook for about 1½ hours for medium. Baste the meat halfway through cooking. If the vegetables look dry add a little water.

3. If you want to make roast potatoes or other vegetables remember to do these while the beef is cooking.

4. When the beef is cooked to your liking, remove the tray from the oven and transfer to a board, cover with tinfoil to rest for 15 minutes while you make gravy (*see page 56*) or finish any accompanying vegetables. Slice the beef and serve with a selection of the roasted vegetables and other vegetables of your choice.

ROAST SILVERSIDE OF SCOTCH BEEF PGI
WITH ROAST RED ONION AND GARLIC

SERVES: **6** PREP: **20 mins** COOK: **2 hrs 35 mins**

INGREDIENTS

2kg boned and rolled Scotch Beef PGI silverside

1 tbsp beef dripping or butter

Salt and black pepper

8-12 small red onions, peeled and slit in a cross at the pointed end (so that they do not burst in the oven)

4 heads garlic, halved

A few sprigs of thyme

METHOD

1. Preheat the oven to 220°C. Rub the rolled silverside joint with the beef dripping and sprinkle with plenty of salt and pepper. Put the joint into a roasting tin and into the hot oven for 15 minutes to brown.

2. Reduce the oven temperature to 180°C. Add the onions, garlic and thyme around the beef with about 100ml of water. Cover with foil and cook for about 1½ hours for medium (*see timings for guidance, page 35*), basting from time to time and adding a little more water if necessary. This will keep the meat moist. Re-cover with the foil each time.

3. Uncover the meat for the last 15 minutes of cooking.

4. Remove the meat to a warm serving dish to rest with the onions and garlic, cover well and keep it warm.

5. Slice the beef and serve a couple of slices per person with the soft onions, a piece of garlic and your choice of vegetables.

ROAST RIB OF SCOTCH BEEF PGI

SERVES: **10**   PREP: **20 mins**   COOK: **2 hr 30 mins**

INGREDIENTS

3kg rib of Scotch Beef PGI on the bone

2 tbsp olive oil

1kg shallots peeled and halved lengthwise

3 heads garlic, cut in half widthwise

Juice of 2 oranges

3 tbsp wholegrain mustard

3 tbsp light muscovado sugar

Leaves from 6 sprigs of thyme

2 tsp coarse flakes of salt

Freshly ground black pepper

Finely grated zest of ½ orange

METHOD

1. Preheat the oven to 220°C. Weigh the joint and calculate the cooking time (*see timings for guidance, page 35*).

2. In a large roasting tin, toss the shallots and garlic with the oil and roast for 15 minutes. Pour the orange juice over the shallots.

3. Meanwhile, with a very sharp knife score a criss-cross pattern deeply into the fat of the beef, but not through to the flesh. Mix together the mustard, sugar, thyme, salt, pepper and orange zest and rub this mixture all over the beef but particularly between the cuts. Set the beef on top of the shallots and return to the oven. After 15 minutes, reduce the oven temperature to 190°C.

4. Check every now and again that the beef is not browning too quickly and that the shallots and garlic are slightly moist, add 100ml of water if necessary, and cover the beef loosely with a double sheet of greaseproof paper. Once cooked allow the meat to rest covered with foil for 15 minutes, in a warm place, before carving thinly. Serve with the soft shallots and vegetables of your choice.

YORKSHIRE PUDDINGS

SERVES: **12**   PREP: **15-20 mins**   COOK: **20 mins**

INGREDIENTS

225g plain flour

Pinch salt

2 medium eggs

300ml milk mixed with 200ml water

Sunflower oil

12 hole muffin tin for the puds

METHOD

1. In a large bowl mix the flour and salt. Make a well in the centre and break in the eggs. Whisk in half the liquid, gradually incorporating the flour as you whisk until you have a smooth thick batter with no lumps. Stir in the remaining liquid and leave to stand for 10 minutes.

2. Put $\frac{1}{2}$ a teaspoon of sunflower oil into each of the muffin cups and place the muffin tin in the oven until very hot.

3. Stir the batter well, then $\frac{2}{3}$ fill each muffin cup and return to the oven for about 20 minutes until well risen and golden brown. They should feel firm and in no danger of collapsing. Leave them in a little longer if necessary.

Tasty Tip:
If you have problems with soggy bottoms on your Yorkshire puds then try this: add $\frac{1}{3}$ of the batter to the hot oil in each muffin cup and place in the oven until they start to rise, about 5 minutes, then add the remaining batter to each cup and return to the oven for the last 15 minutes or so.

BEEF GRAVY

SERVES: **6-8**   PREP: **2 mins**   COOK: **10 mins**

INGREDIENTS

Beef roasting tray (just after joint removed)

2 tbsp plain flour

1 tsp of English/Dijon mustard or mustard powder

750ml hot beef or vegetable stock

2-3 sprigs of fresh herbs (bay leaf, thyme or rosemary), optional

This is a simple but tasty gravy recipe. It can be varied by adding a splash of red wine, balsamic vinegar or a spoonful of red currant jelly, to suit your taste.

METHOD

1. Spoon off and discard excess fat from the tray, leaving just enough to absorb the flour.

2. Set the tray on the stove and add the flour and mustard.

3. Stir to make a smooth paste. Cook for a minute before gradually adding the stock (don't worry if it's lumpy).

4. Continue to stir until the gravy is smooth and thickened. Season to taste. Add more stock or water if too thick or continue to simmer to thicken. Pour the gravy through a sieve if you want it smooth. Serve in a warm jug.

LEFTOVER RECIPES

MEDITERRANEAN ROASTED FIELD MUSHROOMS

SERVES: **4**   PREP: **15 mins**   COOK: **30 mins**

INGREDIENTS

125g cooked Scotch Beef PGI, shredded

4 large field mushrooms

2-3 tbsp olive oil

1 shallot, finely chopped

1 garlic clove, finely chopped

4 sunblush tomatoes, finely chopped

4 tbsp chopped fresh parsley

50g soft cream cheese or mascarpone

50g fresh white breadcrumbs

2 tbsp freshly grated Parmesan

Leafy green salad, to serve

METHOD

1. Heat oven to 200°C. Cut the stems from the mushrooms and chop finely.

2. Heat a tablespoon of oil in a small pan and cook the mushroom stalks, shallot and garlic for 3-4 minutes until softened. Place in a bowl with the sunblush tomatoes, beef, most of the parsley and the soft cheese and mix together until the beef is evenly coated.

3. Lightly brush the outside of the mushroom caps with oil and sit gill-side up on a baking sheet. Divide the beef mixture between the mushrooms.

4. Mix together the breadcrumbs, Parmesan, remaining tablespoon of chopped parsley and a teaspoon of olive oil. Sprinkle evenly over the mushrooms and bake for 15-20 minutes until the mushrooms are tender and the topping is crunchy and golden. Serve warm with a leafy green salad.

BEEF AND BLACK BEAN CHILLI

SERVES: 4 PREP: **10 mins** COOK: **30 mins**

INGREDIENTS

300g cooked Scotch Beef PGI, shredded

1-2 tbsp olive oil

1 onion, chopped

2 red chillies, chopped

1 tbsp smoked paprika

1 tsp ground cumin

400g can chopped tomatoes

400g can black beans, drained and rinsed

1 tbsp wine vinegar

2 tsp brown sugar

4 tbsp chopped coriander

Tortilla chips, soured cream, grated cheese, to serve

METHOD

1. Heat the oil in a large pan and cook the onion and chilli for 5 minutes until softened. Add the paprika and cumin and cook for a minute more. Stir in the beef and tomatoes, cover and cook for 15 minutes. Check the seasoning.

2. Stir in the beans, vinegar, sugar and a splash of water and cook for a further 10 minutes. Divide between bowls and scatter over the coriander.

3. Serve with tortilla chips, soured cream and grated cheese.

BEEF AND BARLEY SOUP

SERVES: **4** PREP: **5 mins** COOK: **40 mins**

INGREDIENTS

300g cooked Scotch Beef PGI, shredded

2 tbsp olive oil

Knob of butter

3 onions, thinly sliced

4 thyme sprigs

75g pearl barley

1 litre beef stock

½ a Savoy cabbage, shredded

METHOD

1. Heat the oil and butter in a large pan and cook the onions and thyme for 15 minutes until dark golden.

2. Add the pearl barley, beef and stock, bring to the boil and simmer for 20 minutes or until the barley is tender.

3. Add the cabbage and cook for a further 3-4 minutes.

4. Ladle the soup into bowls.

MINI TOAD IN THE HOLES

MAKES: **12**   PREP: **15 mins**   COOK: **25 mins**

INGREDIENTS

250g cooked Scotch Beef PGI, cubed

200g plain flour

½ tsp English mustard powder

Pinch of salt

3 eggs

300ml milk

2 tbsp olive oil

4 spring onions, thinly sliced

METHOD

1. Place the flour, mustard and salt in a bowl and stir in the eggs, followed by the milk. Swap your wooden spoon for a wire whisk and beat until smooth. Cover and chill for 10 minutes or until ready to cook.

2. Heat oven to 220°C. Divide the oil between a 12-hole muffin or deep tartlet tin and heat in the oven for 5 minutes.

3. Stir the beef and spring onions into the batter. Quickly ladle into the heated tin and bake for 20-25 minutes until well risen and browned – make sure they are cooked all the way through or they will sink as they cool.

4. Serve with sour cream and chives.

Tasty Tip:
If you have problems with soggy bottoms on your mini toads then try this: add ⅓ of the batter to the hot oil in each muffin cup and place in the oven until they start to rise, about 5 minutes, then add the remaining batter to each cup and return to the oven for the last 15 minutes or so.

STOVIES

SERVES: **4** PREP: **15 mins** COOK: **40 mins**

INGREDIENTS

300g cooked Scotch Beef PGI, diced

1 tbsp sunflower oil

Knob of butter

1kg white potatoes, thinly sliced

1 large onion, thinly sliced

450ml beef stock

Freshly grated nutmeg

4 tbsp finely chopped parsley or chives

METHOD

1. Heat the oil and butter in a large pan and layer up the potatoes, onion and beef, seasoning and sprinkling with nutmeg and herbs as you go.

2. Pour over the stock, cover and cook for 30-40 minutes, shaking the pan from time to time until the potatoes are cooked through (the ones at the bottom will be soft and the ones at the top, just tender). Sprinkle over some herbs and black pepper and serve.

EVERYDAY RECIPES

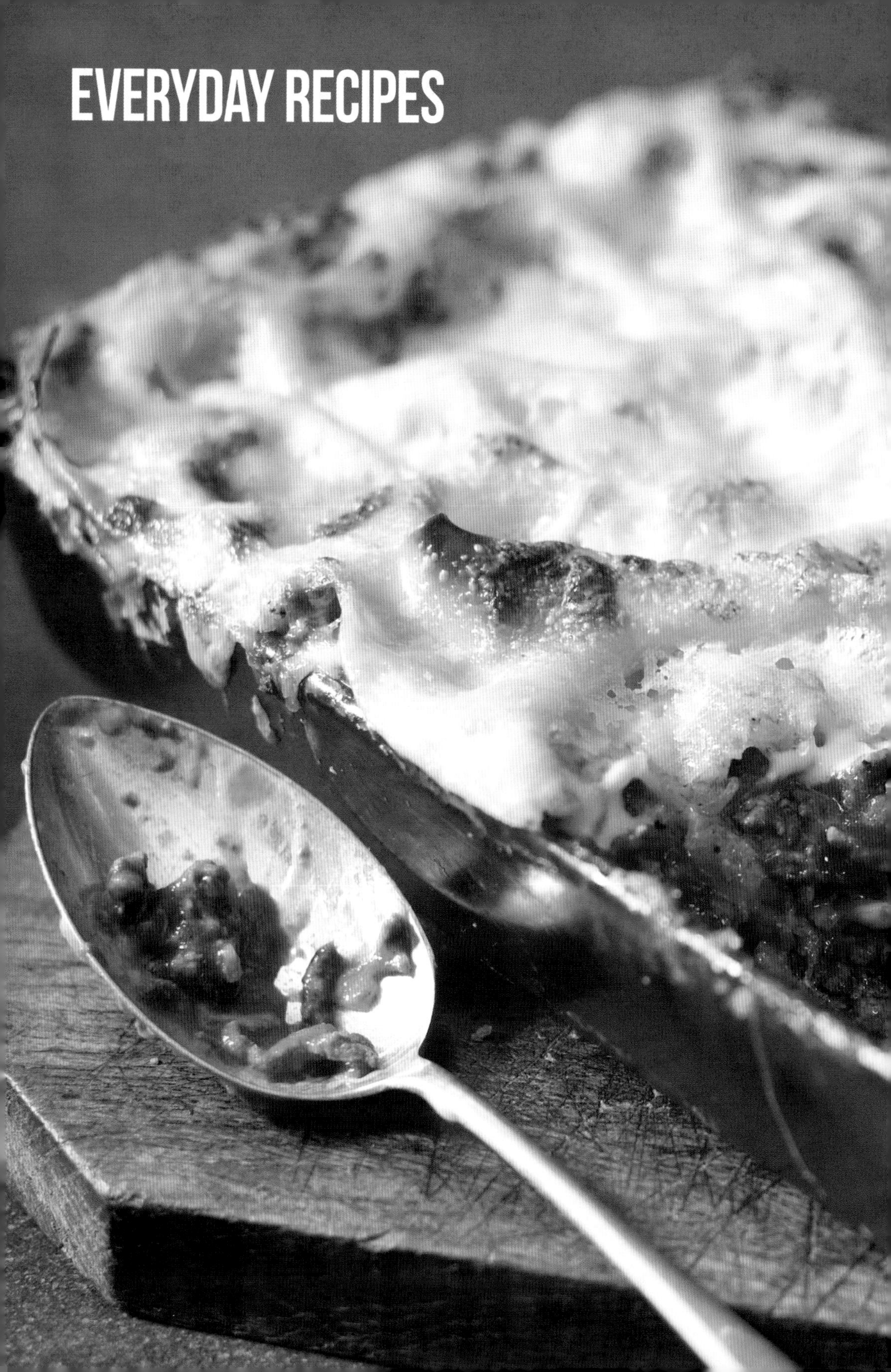

LASAGNE AL FORNO

SERVES: **6** PREP: **15 mins** COOK: **1 hr 45 mins**

INGREDIENTS

750g Scotch Beef PGI mince

4 rashers smoked streaky bacon, chopped

1 tbsp olive oil

1 onion, chopped

1 garlic clove, chopped

2 celery stalks, chopped

2 cans chopped tomatoes

300ml red wine or beef stock

2 bay leaves

375g packet dried lasagne sheets

500g jar white béchamel sauce

220g ball mozzarella, drained and roughly torn

2 tbsp freshly grated Parmesan

METHOD

1. Heat the oil in large pan and cook the onion, garlic, celery and bacon over a fairly high heat until nicely browned. Add the beef and continue to cook the meat to seal it all over.

2. Add the tomatoes, wine or stock and bay leaves. Bring to the boil then cover and simmer for 45 minutes.

3. Heat the oven to 190°C. Spread a third of the meat sauce into a large baking dish and top with a layer of lasagne. Add a little white sauce and some mozzarella then continue to layer up to make three layers finishing with the lasagne sheets topped with white sauce. Scatter over the remaining mozzarella and sprinkle evenly with Parmesan.

4. Cook in the oven for 45 minutes, covering with foil once the top is nicely browned. Leave to sit for a few minutes before serving.

BEEF CARBONNADE

SERVES: **4-6**   PREP: **20 mins**   COOK: **2 hrs**

INGREDIENTS

675g lean Scotch Beef PGI braising steak, cut into 1.25cm cubes

3 tbsp flour, seasoned with black pepper and salt

1 tbsp oil

2 onions, peeled and sliced

1 clove garlic, crushed

1 tbsp tomato purèe

1 tbsp English mustard

300ml brown ale

300ml stock

1 tsp brown sugar

1 bouquet garni

Black pepper

2 carrots, peeled and cut into chunks

2 parsnips, peeled and cut into chunks

Garlic and Herb Croutons

Half a French stick, sliced into 8

25g butter or margarine

1-2 cloves garlic, crushed

1 tbsp fresh parsley, chopped

METHOD

1. Preheat the oven to 170°C.

2. Coat the beef in the seasoned flour. Heat the oil in an ovenproof casserole and brown the beef. Add the onions and garlic and cook for 2-3 minutes. Add all remaining ingredients. Bring to the boil, cover and cook in the preheated oven, for 1½-2 hours.

3. To make the garlic and herb croutons in a small bowl, mix the butter or margarine with the garlic and herbs. Lightly toast one side of the sliced bread. Spread the garlic and herb mixture on the other side and toast until golden.

4. Serve the carbonnade piled into a bowl with croutons and steamed cabbage.

BEEF GOULASH

SERVES: **2-3**   PREP: **10 mins**   COOK: **25-35 mins**

INGREDIENTS

300g Scotch Beef PGI rump or minute steaks, cut into strips

300g new or waxy potatoes, thickly sliced

1 tbsp olive oil

100g button mushrooms, halved

1 small green pepper, finely sliced

1 onion, finely sliced

2 tsp paprika

500g jar tomato based cooking sauce

300ml hot beef stock

2 tbsp natural yoghurt

Freshly chopped parsley or chives (optional)

METHOD

1. Blanch the potatoes in boiling water for 3-4 minutes then drain thoroughly. Meanwhile heat the oil in a wok or large frying pan and stir-fry the beef for 2-3 minutes or until browned.

2. Add the mushrooms, pepper, onion, paprika and potato slices and cook for a further minute.

3. Stir in the tomato sauce and stock, leave to gently simmer for 10 minutes – longer to reduce and thicken the sauce if preferred.

4. Serve in bowls topped with a spoonful of yoghurt and fresh herbs or a dusting of paprika.

Tasty Tip:
For a slow cook Goulash, use Scotch Beef PGI shoulder or featherblade, cubed and cooked with the above ingredients in a lidded casserole for 2½ hours at 140°C. Add a little more stock if required halfway through cooking.

BEEF RATATOUILLE

SERVES: **3-4** PREP: **20 mins** COOK: **2 hrs 30 mins (approx)**

INGREDIENTS

450g lean Scotch Beef PGI braising steak, cut into chunky cubes

1 tbsp olive oil

1 onion, peeled and cut into chunks

2 cloves garlic, crushed

400g can chopped tomatoes

1 tsp dried mixed herbs

150ml stock

1 red pepper, deseeded and cut into large chunks

1 green pepper, deseeded and cut into large chunks

1 courgette, cut into large chunks

1 small aubergine, cut into large chunks

Black pepper

METHOD

1. Preheat the oven to 180°C.

2. In a large ovenproof dish heat the oil and brown the beef in batches then put it all back in the dish.

3. Add the onion, garlic, chopped tomatoes, herbs and stock. Stir and place in a the oven for 1-1½ hours.

4. Remove the casserole from the oven and stir in the vegetables. Season and return to the oven for 30-60 minutes, until the vegetables are soft and the meat is tender.

5. Serve piled on a plate with boiled rice and additional vegetables.

MEATBALLS

SERVES: 4   PREP: **20 mins**   COOK: **40 mins**

INGREDIENTS

For the meatballs

600g Scotch Beef PGI mince

1 small onion, finely chopped

2 tbsp fresh breadcrumbs

2 tbsp cream

1 egg yolk

1 tbsp finely chopped parsley or chives

1 tsp chopped rosemary

Salt and pepper

2 tbsp olive oil

For the tomato sauce

750g large ripe tomatoes, skinned and coarsely chopped

1 large onion, peeled and finely chopped

2 cloves garlic, crushed

2 tbsp olive oil

100ml red wine

100ml water

2 tsp oregano, chopped

Salt and pepper

1 tsp sugar (optional)

To serve

500g fresh pappardelle (or 300g if dried pasta)

1 tbsp finely chopped flat leaf parsley

A little olive oil

A chunk of fresh Parmesan to grate

METHOD

1. Mix together all the meatball ingredients except the oil, then with wet hands, roll the mixture into walnut sized balls. Set aside to chill while you prepare the sauce.

2. Heat a large deep sauté pan over a low heat and fry the onions and garlic in the oil until soft and just beginning to brown (6 minutes). Add the tomatoes and oregano, stir, then cook a minute more before adding the wine and water. Bring to the boil and reduce the heat and simmer gently for about 15 minutes until thick and pulpy. Add a little more water if necessary, then season with salt and pepper and if the sauce is a little sour, add some sugar and taste again until just right for you.

3. Heat the olive oil in a large shallow pan and fry the meatballs until brown all over. Lift and dry on kitchen paper.

4. Add the meatballs to the sauce, stir gently through and cook for about 10 minutes. Serve with pasta, parsley and grated Parmesan.

RATHER SPECIAL BURGER

SERVES: 4   PREP: **25 mins**   COOK: **30 mins**

INGREDIENTS

600g lean Scotch Beef PGI mince

Small red onion, finely chopped

2 tbsp chopped herbs such as parsley, chives, marjoram

4 ciabatta buns, (olive ones are very good)

For caramelized onions

3 medium red onions, peeled and thinly sliced

25g unsalted butter

2 tbsp olive oil

Pinch of salt

Pinch of sugar

To serve

Mixed baby salad leaves

1 large tomato, cut into 8 slices

METHOD

1. Start with the caramelized onions. Fry the onions in the oil and butter over a gentle heat until transparent and soft (6 minutes) then sprinkle on the salt and sugar and continue cooking, stirring from time to time until golden and sticky and beginning to crisp at the edges. Set aside.

2. Mix together all the burger ingredients and season. Mixing them with your hands makes it easier. Shape into four burgers about 10-12 cm diameter.

3. Light the BBQ or heat the grill to its hottest setting and cook the burgers for 3-4 minutes on each side for rare, 4-5 minutes for medium and 5-6 minutes for well done.

4. Pop the split ciabatta buns under the grill to warm a little.

5. Load up the buns with a handful of salad leaves, a couple of tomato slices, a burger and a tangle of onions.

BEEF CASSEROLE

SERVES: **6**   PREP: **15 mins**   COOK: **2 hrs**

INGREDIENTS

1kg Scotch Beef PGI braising steak, cut into large pieces

3 tbsp plain flour, seasoned with salt and pepper

2 tbsp vegetable oil

70g chopped pancetta or smoked bacon

18 whole shallots, peeled

500g small whole carrots, scrubbed and trimmed

3 sticks celery, cut into 3cm lengths

6 small turnips scrubbed and halved

2 cloves garlic, finely chopped

400g can chopped tomatoes

500ml beef stock

300ml ale or stout (optional)

Small bundle herbs tied with string e.g. thyme, parsley and bay leaf

METHOD

1. Preheat the oven to 170°C. Toss the beef pieces in seasoned flour and fry in the oil in batches until well browned on both sides, remove with a slotted spoon to an oven-proof casserole dish.

2. Add the pancetta to the pan and cook until the fat runs, add the shallots and fry gently for 5-8 minutes until starting to brown, then add carrots, celery and turnips and continue cooking for a further 10 minutes, browning gently.

3. Add the garlic and tomatoes and stir together for 2-3 minutes and transfer all this to the casserole with the meat before pouring in the stock, ale (if using) and herbs. Bring to the boil then cover the pot and cook in the oven for about 1½ hours until all is tender and the juices are rich and delicious. Remove the herbs and check the seasoning.

4. Serve with mashed or boiled potatoes and a sprinkle of fresh parsley.

ENTERTAINING RECIPES

STEAK AND MUSHROOM PIE

SERVES: 8 PREP: **20 mins** COOK: **3 hrs**

INGREDIENTS

1.5kg Scotch Beef PGI braising steak cut into 3cm cubes

20g dried mixed wild mushrooms, soaked in 200ml boiling water

3 tbsp plain flour seasoned with salt and pepper

3 tbsp vegetable oil

3 medium onions, peeled and thickly sliced

6-8 large flat mushrooms cut into quarters

1 litre hot beef stock (made from cubes if you wish)

3 sprigs thyme

1 bay leaf

For the topping

500g ready-made puff pastry

1 small egg, beaten (to glaze)

METHOD

1. Preheat the oven to 170°C. In a small bowl cover the dried mushrooms with 200ml boiling water, set aside. Heat some of the oil in a deep sauté pan and gently fry the onions for 5-10 minutes till softened then with a slotted spoon transfer to an oven-proof casserole.

2. Toss the cubed meat in the seasoned flour, shake off any excess then fry the meat in the remaining oil in the pan, you will need to do this in batches, using a little more oil as necessary, until all the beef is well browned.

3. Pour the beef stock and the mushroom soaking liquid into the frying pan and stir to gather up all the sticky bits from the bottom. Pour this mixture over the beef in the casserole dish along with the soaked mushrooms, thyme and bay leaf. Bring to the boil then cover with a lid and cook in the oven for about 1½ hours or until the meat is tender. Adjust the seasoning if necessary.

4. Lightly sauté the quartered mushrooms in a little oil and set them aside until the meat is cooked.

5. Stir the mushrooms into the meat mixture then spoon it into a 2 litre traditional pie dish with only a minimum of the gravy and allow the meat to cool completely. If the gravy is thin, set the casserole over a medium heat, bring back to the boil then simmer for 5-10 minutes without the lid for the gravy to reduce and thicken. Spoon some of this into the pie dish to just sufficiently coat the meat and reserve the rest to serve with the pie.

6. When the meat is cool, set the oven to 200°C. Roll out the pastry to the thickness of a pound coin. Cut two strips to stick to the rim of the pie dish, stick by wetting the rim with water and placing the strips of pastry to cover it. Then cover the whole dish with pastry, moistening the base of the edge of the pastry first, and press to seal all round with the side of your thumb. Trim off any excess pastry and use to decorate the top of the pie. Lightly brush with the beaten egg, pierce a hole in the top with a sharp knife, to allow steam to escape, then cook for about 50 minutes until the pastry is nicely risen and golden brown, and the filling piping hot. Reduce the oven temperature to 180°C after the first 15-20 minutes of cooking.

7. Cover the pie loosely with a double sheet of baking parchment if you feel the pastry is browning too quickly.

8. Serve with lightly buttered steamed cabbage and the reserved gravy, heated.

PULLED SPICED BEEF BRISKET

SERVES: **8**   PREP: **20 mins**   COOK: **4 hrs**

INGREDIENTS

1kg Scotch Beef PGI brisket

A little olive oil (to brush over the rubbed beef)

For the rub

2 tsp chilli flakes

1 tbsp smoked paprika

1 tsp coarse ground black pepper

1 tsp salt flakes

1 tsp dried oregano

For the vegetable base

1 tbsp olive oil

2 onions, thickly sliced

4 sweet peppers, deseeded and cut in quarters

2 cloves garlic, thinly sliced

400g can chopped tomatoes

400ml beef or vegetable stock

1 bay leaf

For the relish

2 ripe avocados, peeled and cut into small cubes

2 tomatoes, finely diced

1 small red onion, finely chopped

1 large red chilli, deseeded and finely chopped

Juice of 1 lime

1 tbsp olive oil

2 tbsp coarsely chopped coriander leaf

Taco shells or rice

Soured cream or Greek-style yogurt

METHOD

1. Score the brisket all over with a sharp knife, or ask the butcher to do it for you.

2. Pound together all the rub ingredients in a mortar and pestle then rub this mixture all over the beef. Set aside.

3. For the vegetable layer, fry the onions gently with the olive oil for about 5 minutes until softened but not brown. Add the rest of the prepared vegetables and stir all together for a couple of minutes, add the tomatoes, stock and the bay leaf and bring to the boil.

4. Brush the meat with the olive oil and brown over a high heat in a heavy-based pan, then sit it on top of the vegetables, cover with the lid, reduce the heat to its lowest setting and cook over a very gentle heat on the hob (or in the oven at about 160°C) for 3-3½ hours. Check the liquid levels in the pan from time to time so that it doesn't boil dry.

5. Prepare the relish by mixing all the ingredients together in a bowl.

6. When the meat is ready you will be able to pull it apart into strands using two large forks. Remove the meat from the pan, shred it as described and keep it warm while you check the seasoning of the vegetables. If there is too much liquid around the vegetables, boil a little more until the juices are syrupy.

7. Using either the tacos or some rice as the base, spoon on some of the soft vegetables, then some of the 'pulled' beef and top with avocado relish and soured cream or yogurt.

CHILLI BASIL KEBABS

SERVES: **2**   PREP: **15-20 mins**   COOK: **20 mins (approx)**

INGREDIENTS

450g lean Scotch Beef PGI popeseye (rump) steaks, cut into small cubes

2-3 red or yellow peppers chopped into chunks

4 tbsp fresh basil, roughly torn

2 cloves garlic, crushed

2 tbsp sweet chilli sauce

1 green or red chilli, deseeded and chopped

150g dried egg noodles

METHOD

1. In a bowl, mix together all the ingredients except the beef, peppers and noodles. Keep aside a little of the marinade to use later.

2. Add the beef and peppers to the marinade, mix thoroughly, cover and refrigerate. Marinate for approximately 30 minutes to 4 hours.

3. Thread the meat and peppers on to skewers. Cook under a preheated grill or barbecue for approximately 12-15 minutes, turning occasionally.

4. Meanwhile, in a saucepan cook the noodles as per packet instructions. Heat the remaining marinade in the pan and boil for 3-4 minutes until piping hot. Add the noodles and mix.

5. Serve the kebabs and noodles immediately with extra stir-fried vegetables or with mixed salad leaves.

BEEF CARPACCIO TARTLETS

SERVES: **4**   PREP: **30 mins**   COOK: **20 mins**

INGREDIENTS

450g piece of Scotch Beef PGI fillet, trimmed of any fat and sinew

2 tsp mixed peppercorns, pounded in a mortar and pestle

1 tbsp rosemary, finely chopped

2 pinches salt

1 small raw beetroot, peeled

1 medium carrot, peeled

100g celeriac, peeled

2 tbsp extra virgin olive oil

2 tbsp balsamic vinegar

Salt

Hot horseradish sauce

8 small basil leaves

For the tartlets

200g plain flour

100g cold, unsalted butter, cut into cubes

25g finely grated Parmesan

2 tbsp cold water

10cm mini tart tins, buttered

METHOD

1. Make the pastry, put the flour, butter and cheese in a food processor and pulse until fine breadcrumbs, add the water and pulse to combine. Remove from the processor and pinch together with your fingers, chill.

2. Mix the pepper, rosemary and salt together on a flat surface then roll the beef firmly over to coat the surface. Heat a griddle to very hot and brown the meat on all sides, 5-6 minutes. Remove to a board to cool.

3. Heat the oven to 200°C and place a baking sheet on the middle shelf.

4. Thinly roll out the pastry and line the mini tins. Prick the pastry bases with a fork and press some buttered foil into the cases to prevent the pastry sliding whilst cooking. Bake for 10 minutes, remove the foil and finish cooking for 10 minutes until crisp and golden. Cool a little before placing on a cooling rack.

5. Cut the vegetables into very fine julienne strips with a mandolin grater or by hand into matchsticks, keep them in three piles. In a bowl mix the oil, vinegar and salt and set aside.

6. Slice the beef very thinly. Carefully arrange a couple of slices into each pastry case with a pile of vegetable sticks. Add some dressing and horseradish then top each with a basil leaf.

CRISPY BEEF IN BEER BATTER

SERVES: **2**   PREP: **10 mins**   COOK: **15 mins**

INGREDIENTS

450g Scotch Beef PGI rump steak

100g self-raising flour

2 tsp mustard powder

150ml beer or lager

1 tsp fine sea salt and pepper

Vegetable oil for deep frying

Tomato ketchup to serve

METHOD

1. Trim the steak of all fat and slice into 1cm strips. In a shallow bowl mix 1 tablespoon flour with the mustard and a little salt and pepper.

2. Put the remaining flour and salt in a small mixing bowl, make a well in the centre and gradually whisk in the beer to make a smooth batter.

3. Heat a pan with about 5-6cm of oil to 180°C. Toss the steak slices into the mustard flour and shake off any excess, then dip each slice into the batter and cook in the hot oil for about 3 minutes until crisp and golden brown, not more than 5 or 6 pieces at a time. Remove with a slotted spoon and drain on a baking tray lined with plenty of kitchen paper. Keep them warm while you cook the rest, making sure that the oil reaches 180°C before adding the next batch.

4. Serve in a bowl freshly lined with absorbent paper and a pot of ketchup for dipping.

CHINESE BEEF DUMPLINGS

SERVES: 4   PREP: **45 mins**   COOK: **15 mins**

INGREDIENTS

500g Scotch Beef PGI mince

2 tbsp sunflower oil

2 garlic cloves, crushed

1 tsp finely grated ginger

2 small red chillies, deseeded and finely chopped

2 tbsp oyster sauce (light soy sauce can be used as a substitute)

275g packet dumpling wrappers (available from Chinese/Oriental supermarkets)

3 spring onions, shredded

1 tbsp sesame oil

Dipping Sauce

4 tbsp soy sauce

Juice of 1 lime

2 tsp toasted sesame seeds

METHOD

1. Heat one tablespoon of the sunflower oil in wok and stir fry the mince, garlic, ginger and half the chilli for 5 minutes or until just cooked. Stir in the oyster sauce and set aside for 10 minutes to cool.

2. Spoon a teaspoon of the mixture into centre of a wrapper. Brush the edge with water and fold the pastry over to enclose filling. Pleat the edges together firmly to seal then repeat to make a total of 24 dumplings.

3. Poach the dumplings in simmering water a few at a time for about 30 seconds or so until they float to the surface. Remove with a slotted spoon and cover to keep warm while cooking remaining dumplings.

4. Heat the remaining sunflower oil and the sesame oil in a frying pan and cook the spring onions and remaining chilli together for a minute or so until turning golden.

5. Mix together the soy sauce, lime juice and sesame seeds and pour into a small dipping bowl.

6. Arrange the dumplings on plates and scatter over the spring onion mixture and serve with the dipping sauce.

Cook's tip: To make your own dumpling wrappers, place 300g plain flour in a food processor then with the motor running, slowly pour in 100-125ml just boiled water to make a fairly soft dough. Shape into small balls then roll out thinly on a lightly floured surface into 8cm rounds.

LUNCH/SNACK RECIPES

PERFECT PASTIES

SERVES: **4**   PREP: **25 mins**   COOK: **40 mins**

INGREDIENTS

300g Scotch Beef PGI mince

400g finely diced vegetables
(e.g. carrots, turnip, leek, potato)

1 tsp chopped thyme or ½ tsp dried thyme

Salt and pepper

750g ready made short crust pastry

1 medium egg, beaten with a pinch of salt

METHOD

1. Mix together the vegetables, mince, thyme and season with some salt and plenty of pepper. Set aside.

   Preheat the oven to 180°C. Line a baking sheet with baking parchment. On a separate sheet of baking parchment, lightly dusted with flour, roll out a quarter of the pastry large enough to cut out a 26cm circle of pastry. A dinner plate or fairly large saucepan lid is about that size and is easy to cut around.

2. Spoon about a quarter of the filling mixture onto one side of the pastry round, in a D shape, leaving a 3-4cm border on the curved side to seal and pleat the pastry's edge.

3. Brush some of the egg wash halfway around the circle on the meat side, then carefully, using the paper to help you, fold the pastry over to enclose the filling and press lightly to seal a flat seam.

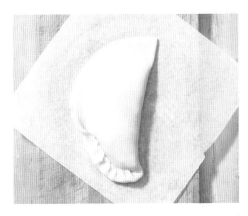

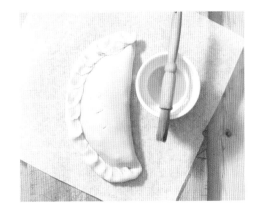

4. Then working from the top of the pastry seam, fold and pleat as you go around the curve making a neat thick edge.

Slide the pasty onto the lined baking sheet and then repeat to make the other three pasties.

5. Brush the pasties all over with the egg wash, pierce two slits in the top of the pasties to allow steam to escape and prevent the pastry from splitting.

Bake in the oven for about 40 minutes until golden brown. Allow to cool for at least 10 minutes before eating.

Serve warm with chutney and mustard.

MEAT LOAF

SERVES: **8** PREP: **15 mins** COOK: **1 hr 30 mins**

INGREDIENTS

1.25 kg lean Scotch Beef PGI mince

3 rashers streaky bacon, roughly chopped

1 onion, peeled and finely chopped

1 stick celery, finely chopped

1 carrot, peeled and grated

2 tbsp finely chopped fresh herbs (e.g. chives, parsley and thyme) or 1 tsp dried mixed herbs

75g sunblush tomatoes, roughly chopped

3 tbsp fresh breadcrumbs

Celery salt and pepper to season

METHOD

1. Preheat the oven to 170°C and oil a large loaf tin.

2. Mix together all the ingredients very thoroughly, season and pack into the loaf tin which has been oiled and lined with foil, spreading evenly and smoothing the top. Cover closely with baking parchment and foil and cook in the oven for about 1½ hours.

3. Remove from the oven and, still covered, leave to stand for at least 30 minutes or until completely cold. It is tastier when it is allowed to cool completely and also easier to slice.

4. You can make a quick gravy with the meat juices and some gravy granules.

5. This is a flexible dish across the seasons. Serve with mashed potatoes, spring greens and steamed leeks if you want a warm meal and a gravy made from the meat juices and some gravy granules, or salad and a jacket potato if you want a summery meal.

BEEF NOODLE SOUP

SERVES: **4**   PREP: **20 mins**   COOK: **15 mins**

INGREDIENTS

250g Scotch Beef PGI fillet (cut from the narrow end), thinly sliced

600ml beef stock

2 tbsp light soy sauce

2 tbsp chilli sauce

2cm piece ginger peeled and cut into matchsticks

2 carrots peeled and cut into matchsticks

100g white button mushrooms, sliced

2 heads pak choi, thinly sliced

Fresh sweetcorn cut from 1 cob

2 bundles rice noodles (about 100g)

4 spring onions, shredded

2 tsp toasted sesame oil

1 tbsp toasted sesame oil to serve

METHOD

1. Into a large broad-based pan pour the stock, soy sauce, chilli sauce and ginger and bring to the boil.

2. Add the carrots and mushrooms and cook for 2 minutes; add the corn and noodles and pak choi and simmer for 3 minutes. Then add the beef slices and shredded onion and heat through to just cook the beef. Stir in the sesame oil and serve the soup in bowls with some sesame seeds sprinkled over each.

BEEF & TOASTED MEXICAN CORNBREAD SANDWICH

SERVES: **4** PREP: **30 mins** COOK: **45 mins (approx)**

INGREDIENTS

For the cornbread

250g yellow cornmeal

85g plain flour

2 tsp baking powder

½ tsp bicarbonate of soda

2 tbsp caster sugar

1 tsp fine sea salt

100g mature cheddar, grated

2 medium eggs, beaten

250ml milk

125ml vegetable oil (sunflower)

3 spring onions, finely chopped

1 medium green chilli, seeded and finely chopped.

1 tsp crushed chilli flakes

Topping

8 slices cold roast beef, shredded into strips

Handful of shredded lettuce

1 ripe avocado, peeled and diced

A little zest and the juice of half a lemon

1 tsp finely chopped red chilli or a dash of hot pepper sauce

Salt and black pepper

4 tsp soured cream

4 tsp chilli and tomato jam

METHOD

1. Preheat the oven to 190°C and grease a 1 litre loaf tin.

2. To make the cornbread, mix together all the dry ingredients and the grated cheese in a large bowl and make a well in the centre.

3. Lightly whisk together the eggs, milk and oil then stir in the onions and chillies.

4. Pour the egg mixture into the dry ingredients and mix lightly with a spoon then pour into the loaf tin. Bake in the oven for about 45-55 minutes until well risen, firm to the touch, crunchy and golden brown. Cool a little in the tin for about 10 minutes then transfer to a cooling rack until cold. (It is delicious to eat when warm but will cut more easily when cold).

5. Toss the avocado with the lemon zest, juice, chilli and season to taste.

6. Heat a griddle pan and toast the cornbread slices until golden brown and crisp.

7. Start with a layer of shredded lettuce, then beef, a pinch of salt, avocado mixture, soured cream and chilli jam. If that is not enough chilli for you, top the whole thing with a preserved jalapeno chilli. Eat with a knife and fork!

STEAK RECIPES

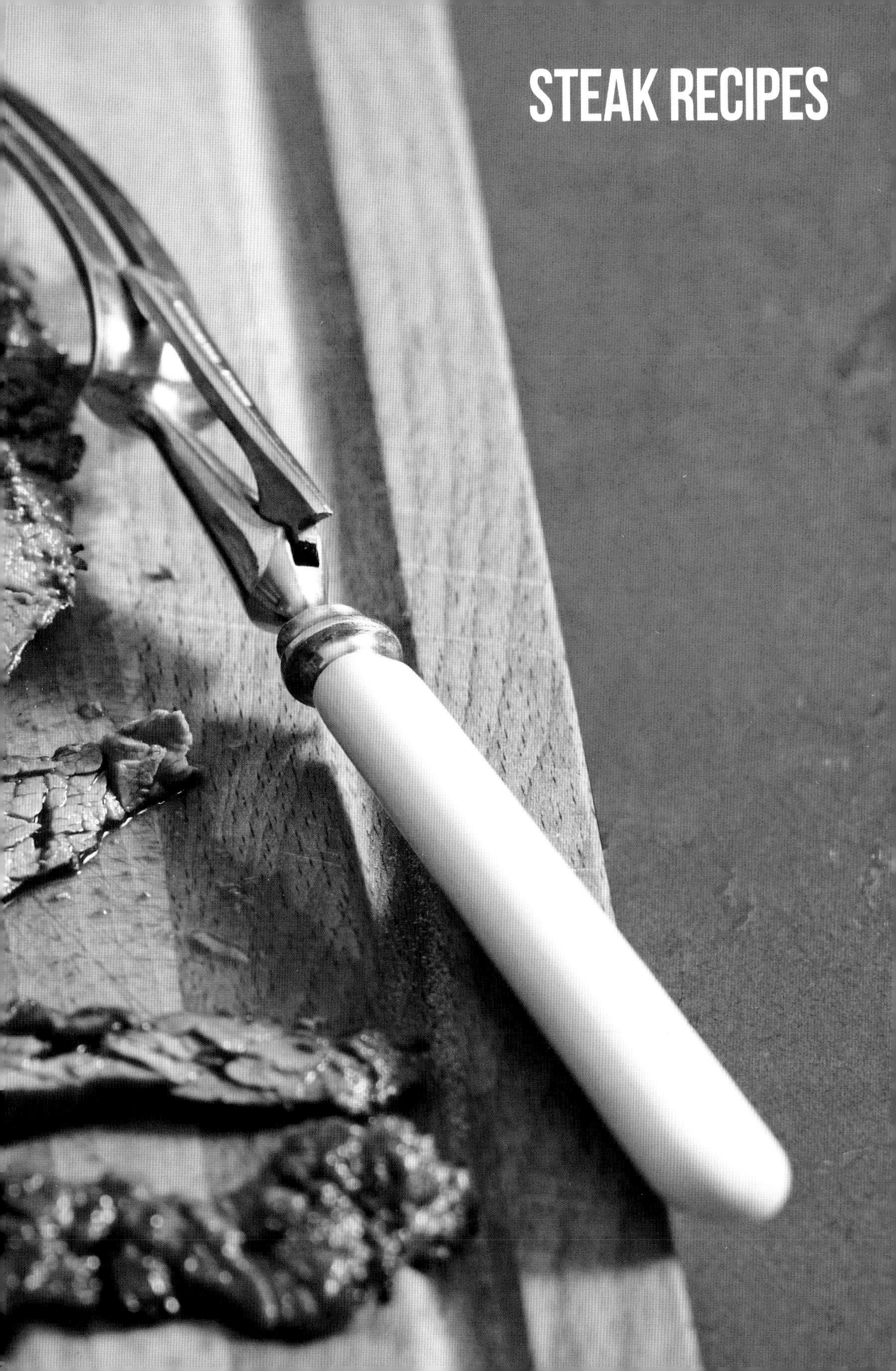

BAVETTE STEAK WITH POTATO WEDGES

SERVES: **6-8**   PREP: **40 mins (including marinating)**   COOK: **35-40 mins**

INGREDIENTS

1.2kg piece Scotch Beef PGI Bavette steak, stripped of membrane and excess fat (ask the butcher to do this for you)

For the marinade

Leaves from 2 sprigs rosemary, finely chopped

Finely grated zest of a small lemon

2 tbsp lemon juice

1 clove garlic, finely chopped

½ tsp salt

2 tbsp olive oil

For the potatoes

6 large potatoes, scrubbed and each cut into 8 wedges

3-4 tbsp sunflower oil

1½ tsp mustard powder

1½ tsp smoked paprika

½ tsp salt

1 tbsp finely chopped rosemary

6-8 small bunches vine cherry tomatoes

Soured cream to serve

METHOD

1. Mix together all the marinade ingredients in a small bowl then brush over the bavette steak, rubbing it well into all the crevices. Set aside to marinate for 20-30 minutes. Get the griddle pan ready (or alternatively, this would work on the BBQ) and set the oven to 210°C.

2. Parboil the potato wedges in fast boiling water for about 5 minutes, drain thoroughly and then toss with the oil, mustard, paprika, salt and rosemary and tip onto a large baking tray in a single layer. Place into the hot oven for about 30 minutes.

3. After 15 minutes turn over the wedges with a spatula. Add the tomatoes to the baking tray for the last 10 minutes of cooking or until the tomato skins are beginning to split and the potatoes are well browned, crisp and tender.

4. Once the Griddle pan is very hot (or the BBQ is at its maximum heat), pat the steak with kitchen paper to absorb any excess moisture then place in the griddle pan or place it on the BBQ until sizzling and brown on one side (about 7 minutes) then turn it over to brown on the other side for a further 5-7 minutes. If the steak is still undercooked and feels too soft to the touch, turn and cook for another couple of minutes on each side. The whole process should take about 15-20 minutes and the steak should be rare to medium/rare. Don't overcook it or it will become tough. Remove the steak to a board, cover with foil to allow it to rest for 5 minutes before carving.

5. When you are ready, carve the meat diagonally against the grain (*see page 40*). Pile it up onto a warm serving dish for people to help themselves along with the potato wedges, tomatoes and a bowl of soured cream.

SIRLOIN STEAK WITH TOMATO & RED ONION SALAD

SERVES: **2**   PREP: **5 mins**   COOK: **10 mins (max)**

INGREDIENTS

2 Scotch Beef PGI sirloin steaks about 200g each

A little olive oil

Salt and pepper

For the salad (optional)

1 small red onion, finely sliced

3-4 ripe tomatoes, finely sliced

A few basil leaves

1 tbsp of olive oil and a squeeze of lemon

METHOD

1. Heat a griddle or frying pan large enough for both steaks. Brush the steaks with a little oil and season with salt and pepper.

2. Cook the steaks for 3-4 minutes each side for medium – see cooking times on page 31 for more details.

3. Rest the steaks for 3 minutes before serving.

4. Whilst the steaks are resting, combine all of the salad ingredients and check for seasoning. Serve the steaks with the salad and a good dollop of mustard.

WARM RUMP STEAK SALAD

SERVES: **2**   PREP: **10 mins**   COOK: **15 mins**

INGREDIENTS

350-400g piece Scotch Beef PGI rump steak, trimmed of excess fat

200g new potatoes, halved if large

100g French beans, trimmed

2 spring onions

2 tomatoes

A handful of mixed salad leaves

For the salad dressing

2 tsp Dijon mustard

1 tsp honey

A pinch each of salt and black pepper

1 tbsp red wine vinegar

2-3 tbsp extra virgin olive oil

METHOD

1. To prepare the salad, wash and dry the leaves and slice the onion and tomatoes.

2. Whisk together all the ingredients for the salad dressing.

3. Boil the potatoes for about 10 minutes until almost tender then throw in the beans and cook for about 4-5 minutes until just tender but with a little bite remaining. Drain well and set aside.

4. While the potatoes are cooking, preheat a griddle pan or grill until very hot. Lightly season the steak then press onto the griddle for about 3-4 minutes (for medium/rare) on each side, or until done to your liking. Rest the steak in a warm place for a few minutes for the fibres to relax and the steak to be its most tender before slicing.

5. Arrange the salad on 2 plates, toss the warm potatoes and beans with half the salad dressing and divide between the plates. Top with slices of the steak, a little more dressing and a sprinkle of spring onion. Serve with chunks of bread to mop up the juices and dressing.

ROCKET SALAD WITH MINUTE STEAK

SERVES: **2** PREP: **10 mins** COOK: **15 mins**

INGREDIENTS

2 Scotch Beef PGI minute steaks
(80-100g each)

Salt and pepper

½ tbsp olive oil

For the salad

80g bag wild rocket salad leaves

½ small red onion, very finely
shredded

2 small peppers, finely sliced
(yellow or green peppers)

For the salad dressing

1 tbsp lemon juice

1 tbsp seeded mustard

2 tbsp good quality olive oil

A little salt and freshly ground black
pepper

25g Parmesan or Grana Padano
cheese

METHOD

1. Put all the salad ingredients into a serving
   bowl. Whisk together all the dressing
   ingredients, except for the cheese, ready
   to dress the salad when the steaks are done.

2. Brush the steaks with a little oil now, then
   cook on a preheated griddle pan or under
   a very hot grill, for 1 minute or less until
   done to your liking.

3. Serve the steak, cut into 3-4 slices piled onto
   the dressed salad. Shave the cheese over the
   top and add a twist of lemon zest or juice and
   enjoy with some crusty warm bread. Or you
   could pack the salad into a warm baguette,
   add sliced steak and Parmesan if you need
   a meal on the go!

RIBEYE STEAK WITH GREEN PEPPERCORN SAUCE

SERVES: **2**   PREP: **10 mins**   COOK: **15 mins**

INGREDIENTS

2 Scotch Beef PGI ribeye steaks, approx 200g each

25g unsalted butter

2-3 tbsp green peppercorns from a jar of green peppercorns in brine

1-2 tbsp brandy

1 clove garlic, crushed with a little salt

2 tsp Dijon mustard

100ml whipping cream

1 tbsp finely chopped parsley

METHOD

1. Lightly salt the fatty edges of the steaks then sear them by holding the two steaks together with tongs and placing on a very hot frying pan until browned and exuding some fat. Manoeuvre the steaks, still together, till the edges are brown all around, then in the rendered fat sear the two separate steaks on both sides until done to your liking. Set the steaks aside in a warm place while you make the sauce.

2. If you want to save washing up, blot up any excess fat from the pan with kitchen paper and re-use it, alternatively you can use a small pan to make the sauce.

3. Melt the butter in the pan until it is foaming.

4. Add the drained peppercorns and crush slightly with the back of a wooden spoon. Add the garlic.

5. Add the brandy and salt and stir together to deglaze the pan, then stir in the mustard and cream.

6. Continue to cook, stirring, until you achieve a nicely thickened sauce that will coat the back of a spoon.

7. Stir in the parsley.

8. Serve the steaks on warmed plates with the sauce spooned over or on the side.

BÉARNAISE SAUCE

SERVES: **4**   *A rich French sauce finished with tarragon*

INGREDIENTS

100ml white wine vinegar

1 shallot, chopped

3 tbsp of tarragon

2 egg yolks, beaten

120g warm melted butter

Salt & pepper

1 tsp lemon juice

METHOD

1. Put the vinegar, shallot, 2 tablespoons of tarragon (keep one for later) and a little salt in a saucepan and boil until reduced by half.

2. Strain into a large bowl and set aside to cool.

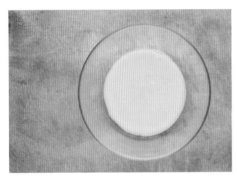

3. Add a teaspoon of water to the beaten egg yolks and add the eggs to the cooled vinegar with the lemon juice.

4. Set the bowl over a pan of barely simmering water and whisk until the egg yolks have thickened enough to coat the back of a spoon.

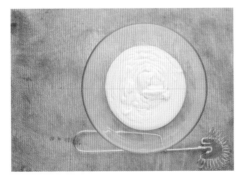

5. Remove the bowl from the heat and slowly pour in the warm melted butter, whisking vigorously as you go. You can use an electric whisk to do this.

6. Once all the butter is added and you have a thick and smooth consistency, stir in the remaining tarragon, season to taste and serve.

CHIMICHURRI SAUCE

A sharp, spicy South American sauce, ideal for steaks

INGREDIENTS

Large bunch (2 big handfuls) of
fresh parsley leaves, chopped

2 tbsp olive oil

1 red chilli, de-seeded and finely
chopped

2-3 garlic cloves, minced or finely
chopped

2 tbsp dried oregano

2-3 tbsp red wine vinegar

$\frac{1}{2}$ tsp sea salt flakes

This sauce is best made the day before as the flavours will intensify.

METHOD

1. Put the chillies and garlic into a bowl and mix together.

2. Add all the other ingredients.

3. Stir well until everything is completely combined.

4. Cover the bowl with cling film and put the mixture in the fridge, ideally overnight or for 2-4 hours to allow the flavours to develop.

To cut down on chopping – if you have a blender you can whizz up all the ingredients for about 10 seconds on a medium speed until blended but not puréed.

SAUCE DIANE

SERVES: **4**   *A classic rich and creamy sauce with mushrooms*

INGREDIENTS

1 tbsp olive oil

1 small onion, finely diced

1 garlic clove, chopped

100g mushrooms, sliced

15g butter

1-2 tbsp Worcestershire sauce

1 tbsp Dijon mustard

50ml brandy or whisky (optional)

200ml double cream

Salt and pepper

After the steaks are cooked and removed from the pan to rest,
use the pan to make the sauce.

METHOD

1. Put a little olive oil in the frying pan, add the onions and fry until soft.

2. Add the garlic, mushrooms, butter and stir for 2 minutes.

3. Add the Worcestershire sauce, mustard, any meat juices from the steak, then stir for a minute.

4. Pour in the alcohol now (if using) turn up the heat and add it to the far end of the pan and allow it to gently ignite. Once the alcohol has burnt off, swirl the juices around the pan.

5. Add the cream and allow the sauce to thicken before turning down the heat.

6. Taste and season as required and serve spooning the sauce over the steaks.

HORSERADISH SAUCE

SERVES: 2-4   *A quick and light sauce made with fresh or jarred horseradish*

INGREDIENTS

1 tbsp grated horseradish, fresh or jarred

2 tbsp low fat natural yoghurt or crème fraiche

Salt and pepper

Squeeze of lemon

2 tsp chopped chives (optional)

METHOD

1. Put the horseradish and yoghurt or crème fraiche into a bowl and add seasoning.

2. Squeeze in the lemon juice and mix thoroughly.

3. Add the chopped chives (if using) and mix again.

4. Taste the sauce; if it is too hot add more yoghurt or more horseradish if you want it hotter.

Take care if grating fresh horseradish root, it can nip your eyes if you get too close.

LEMON & PARSLEY BUTTER

SERVES: 4-6

A zesty, fresh flavoured butter perfect with steaks

INGREDIENTS

100g lightly salted softened butter

1 tsp finely grated lemon zest

1½ tbsp lemon juice

3 tbsp finely chopped parsley

Pepper

The butter will keep for up to 4 days in the fridge and can be frozen.

METHOD

1. Place all the ingredients in a bowl.

2. Blend together all the ingredients and ensure everything is well combined.

3. Shape into a cylinder and roll in cling film.

4. Keep wrapped in cling film and chill until needed then slice.

ALTERNATIVE RECIPE INGREDIENTS

Basil, Parmesan and sun-dried tomato

100g butter

3 tbsp basil leaves (roughly torn)

4 tbsp grated Parmesan

1 tbsp finely chopped sun-dried tomato

Chilli, coriander and lime

100g butter

½ red chill (de-seeded and finely chopped)

2 tbsp fresh coriander leaves (finely chopped)

1 lime (zest only)

Thyme and garlic butter

100g butter

2 tbsp fresh thyme leaves (finely chopped)

2 garlic cloves (minced)

Goats cheese butter

100g butter

100g goats cheese (softened)

1 tbsp fresh parsley (finely chopped)

1 tbsp fresh basil (roughly torn)

SHALLOT & RED WINE SAUCE

SERVES: **2**   *A rich and full flavoured sauce, perfect with steak or red meat*

INGREDIENTS

2 shallots, sliced

1 garlic clove, crushed

Sprig of rosemary or thyme

200ml red wine

200ml stock

½ tsp cornflour mixed with 1 tbsp
of cold water

After the steaks are cooked and removed from the pan to rest,
use the pan to make the sauce.

METHOD

1. Put a little olive oil in the pan, add the shallots and cook until golden (about 2-3 minutes).

2. Now add the garlic and herbs and cook for another few minutes while stirring.

3. Pour in the wine, turn up the heat and scrape up any browned bits from the bottom of the pan. Cook until reduced by two thirds.

4. When reduced, add the stock and the cornflour paste and simmer until the liquid is further reduced and starts to thicken. Remove the herbs.

5. Add the butter and stir through.

6. Add any of the meat juices from the rested steaks and season to taste.

KITCHEN & STORE-CUPBOARD STAPLES

Having the correct equipment to hand will really help. This is not an exhaustive list, just some good to have essentials. Buy the best quality equipment you can, it will be a worthwhile investment as it will last for years.

EQUIPMENT

- Knives – carving knife, a good sharp one, paring knife and serrated knife
- Knife sharpener (knives should be regularly sharpened)
- Carving fork
- Solid block chopping board (good to have separate boards for different foods)
- Oven gloves
- Meat tongs
- Roasting tray (with wire rack) and a baster
- Casserole dish
- Griddle pan
- Frying pan
- Scales
- Timer
- Meat thermometer

Tip: Use the wrong side of your knife to scrape food from the chopping board – never use the blade side!

STORE CUPBOARD STAPLES

Seasoning – black pepper corns, coarse sea salt plus good grinders

A selection of dried herbs and spices (basil, oregano, chilli flakes, paprika, ginger, bay leaves, thyme, garlic salt)

Chopped tomatoes

Worcestershire sauce

Mustard

Soy sauce

Horseradish sauce

Oils – olive or ground nut

Brown sugar

Plain flour

Having some staples in the freezer is also a good idea – frozen vegetables are great as a quick and convenient accompaniment.

CLASSIC BEEF ACCOMPANIMENTS

Beef and horseradish, steak and ale pie, boiled beef and onions – such classic dishes have been around for centuries.

MARINATE

What it does – adds flavour.

What to do – mix marinade ingredients. Place meat and marinade in a plastic bag. Refrigerate.

What to use – horseradish, mustard, red wine, peppercorns, garlic, ginger, wholegrain mustard, brown sugar, allspice, cumin, paprika, wasabi paste, chilli, garlic salt. (These are just few examples, try experimenting with your own marinades).

GLAZE

What it does – adds flavour, enhances visual appeal of cooked meat.

What to do – brush the glaze over the meat a few minutes before end of cooking.

What to use – sugar is essential for glazing. So try blackbean glaze, barbecue sauce or a sweetened wasabi and horseradish.

ACCOMPANIMENTS FOR BEEF

What they do – enhance the meat's natural flavours, enriching each other and the eating experience.

What to do – combine the ingredients and serve with your beef dish.

What to use – for creamy blue cheese, combine natural yoghurt with a good blue vein cheese and chopped spring onions. For a hot chilli accompaniment, mix natural yoghurt, tomatoes and chillis. For the best of British, make some Yorkshire puddings and gravy and serve with horseradish and peppery watercress sauce.

Get boozy! Beef laps up stouts so add your favourite ales in pies and casseroles. Or pan fry and deglaze with Madeira. You can even poach fillet steaks in good red wine and serve with pomme purée and green beans!

PAIRING INGREDIENTS FOR BEEF

Anchovy	Cucumber	Orange
Anise	Dill	Oyster
Artichoke (Jerusalem)	Egg	Parsley
Bacon	French beans	Parsnip
Beetroot	Garlic	Pea
Bell pepper	Ginger	Peanut
Black pudding	Grape	Pear
Blackberry	Haggis	Pepper
Blue cheese	Hard Cheese	Potato
Broccoli	Horseradish	Saffron
Cabbage	Juniper	Shellfish
Caper	Kidney	Swede
Carrot	Lemon	Thyme
Celery	Lime	Tea
Chilli	Liver	Tomato
Cinnamon	Mint	Truffle
Clove	Mushroom	Turnip
Cocoa	Mustard	Walnut
Coconut	Oily fish	Watercress
Coffee	Olives	
Courgette	Onion	

Some interesting flavour combinations to try with Scotch Beef PGI

MORE INFORMATION ABOUT MEAT

Free recipes:
www.scotchbeefkitchen.com

Consumer Clubs – To find member restaurants of the Scotch Beef Club:
www.scotchbeefclub.org

To find members of the Scotch Butchers Club:
www.scotchbutchersclub.org

Food hygiene and general labelling legislation – Food Standards Agency:
www.food.gov.uk

Labelling legislation – search for meat labelling at:
www.scotland.gov.uk

Healthy eating:
www.eatwell.gov.uk

Industry information:
www.qmscotland.co.uk

Scotland Food & Drink:
www.scotlandfoodanddrink.org

Waste of food:
www.lovefoodhatewaste.com

Consumer protection and information – Consumer Focus:
www.consumerfocus-scotland.org.uk

Scottish SPCA – The Scottish Society for the Prevention of Cruelty to Animals:
www.scottishspca.org

PERFECT STEAKS & ROASTS APP

For a *FREE* step by step guide to cooking any cut of meat, download our free
"**Perfect Steaks & Roasts**" app for iPhone, iPod Touch and Android.

Available free from the App Store or Google Play.

Find us on facebook.

INDEX

Campaign
financed
with aid
from the
European
Union.